W9-AHO-149

21st Century Junior Library

Triceratops

by Jennifer Zeiger

CHERRY LAKE PUBLISHING * ANN ARBOR, MICHIGAN

Published in the United States of America by Cherry Lake Publishing
Ann Arbor, Michigan
www.cherrylakepublishing.com

Content Adviser: Gregory M. Erickson, PhD, Dinosaur Paleontologist, Department of Biological
Science, Florida State University, Tallahassee, Florida

Reading Adviser: Marla Conn, ReadAbility, Inc.

Photo Credits: Cover, ©Stocktrek Images, Inc./Alamy; pages 4 and 8, ©MasPix/Alamy; page 6,
©leonello calvetti/Shutterstock, Inc.; page 10, ©Computer Earth/Shutterstock, Inc.; page 12, ©Elina/
Dreamstime.com; page 14, ©AP Photo/Smithsonian National Museum of Natural History; page 16,
©Stocktrek Images, Inc./Alamy; page 18, ©dieKleinert/Alamy; page 20, ©Kumar Sriskandan/Alamy.

LIBRARY OF CONGRESS CATALOGING-IN-PUBLICATION DATA
Zeiger, Jennifer.
  Triceratops/by Jennifer Zeiger.
     p. cm.—(21st century junior library. Dinosaurs and prehistoric animals)
  Audience: K to grade 3.
  Summary: "Learn about the habits of the dinosaur known as Triceratops, from its habits and lifestyle to
its diet and the way it raised its young"—Provided by publisher.
  Includes bibliographical references and index.
  ISBN 978-1-62431-161-1 (lib. bdg.)—ISBN 978-1-62431-227-4 (e-book)—
ISBN 978-1-62431-293-9 (pbk.)
  1. Triceratops—Juvenile literature. 2. Dinosaurs—Juvenile literature. I. Title.
  QE862.O65Z454 2014
  567.915'8—dc23   2013007033

Cherry Lake Publishing would like to acknowledge the work of
The Partnership for 21st Century Skills.
Please visit www.p21.org *for more information.*

Printed in the United States of America
Corporate Graphics Inc.
July 2013
CLFA13

CONTENTS

Tyrannosaurus rex may have been a common predator of *Triceratops*.

What Was Triceratops?

A huge dinosaur moves slowly through the **marsh**. It tears up a bunch of tasty ferns. *Triceratops* raises its head as it chews. It watches for **predators**. Suddenly, a hungry *Tyrannosaurus rex* rushes across the marsh. *Triceratops* has to defend itself. It is ready to fight with its sharp horns.

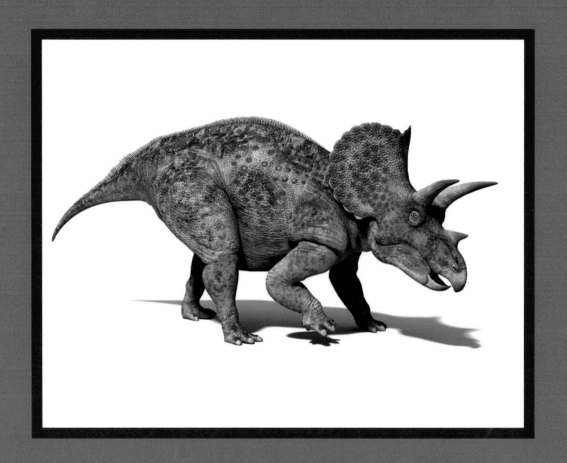

The word *triceratops* means "three-horned face."

Triceratops lived 68 to 65 million years ago. It was found in North America. It was one of the last dinosaurs on Earth. All dinosaurs became **extinct** around 65 million years ago.

Ask Questions! How do scientists know when certain dinosaurs lived? If you don't know the answer, ask! A librarian or teacher can help you find the answer.

Triceratops needed strong, solid legs to move its 6-ton (5,400-kilogram) body.

What Did *Triceratops* Look Like?

Triceratops was very big. An adult weighed more than an elephant does. It was almost as long as a small school bus. The dinosaur's four legs were very strong. This helped them carry the dinosaur's heavy body.

Triceratops's head could be about 10 feet
(3 meters) long.

Triceratops's head was huge. It was among the largest of any land animal ever. It took up one-third of the dinosaur's length. A **frill** stuck out from the back of Triceratops's head. Two long horns were above its eyes. There was another horn on its snout. It was shorter than the others.

Triceratops's beak was quite sharp.

At the end of *Triceratops*'s snout was a beak. This beak curved down. This is much like a parrot's beak today. The dinosaur's mouth was full of teeth. These were behind the dinosaur's beak.

Look!

Take a close look at a picture of *Triceratops*. Does it look like any animals alive today? What animals have horns? Do any have frills on their heads? What kind of animals have beaks?

A *Triceratops* had to protect itself and its territory.

How Did *Triceratops* Live?

Scientists believe *Triceratops* lived alone. It needed to protect its **territory**. It also had to defend itself. The dinosaur was too heavy to run fast. Its horns probably helped the dinosaur fight off predators. They also helped it battle other *Triceratops*. The dinosaurs may have fought over territory or a **mate**.

Triceratops's frill might have been very colorful.

No one is sure why *Triceratops* had a frill. It might have helped protect the dinosaur's neck from attackers.

The frill might also have been for show. The dinosaurs may have known one another by their frills. The frill may also have helped them find a mate.

Create!

Scientists do not know how *Triceratops*'s frill was colored. What color do you guess it was? Draw a picture of *Triceratops*. Color your drawing with crayons or colored pencils.

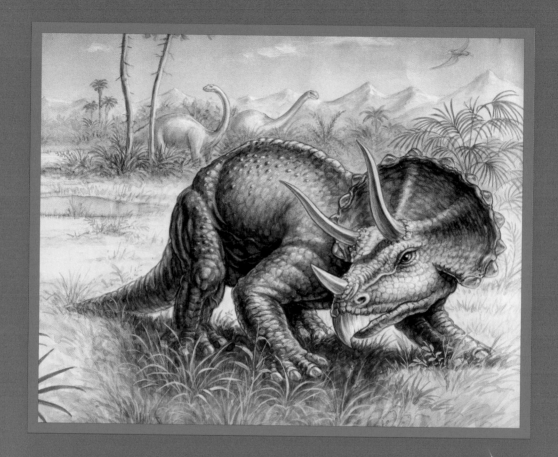

Triceratops was a herbivore, or plant eater.

Plants made up *Triceratops*'s **diet**. The dinosaur mostly ate ferns and other low-growing plants. These plants could be very tough. *Triceratops* cut bites off of them with its sharp beak. Its back teeth were like scissors. They were used to slice up food.

Visitors can see *Triceratops* fossils at museums such as the Smithsonian National Museum of Natural History in Washington, D.C.

We know about *Triceratops* through its **fossils**. These fossils have been found in the United States and Canada. No one has found a complete *Triceratops* **skeleton** yet. Do you want to study dinosaurs? Perhaps one day you will make a big *Triceratops* discovery!

GLOSSARY

diet (DYE-it) the food an animal typically eats

extinct (ik-STINGKT) describing a type of plant or animal that has completely died out

fossils (FAH-suhlz) the preserved remains of living things from thousands or millions of years ago

frill (FRILL) a structure made of bone, feathers, or fur sticking out over the neck of an animal

marsh (MAHRSH) an area of wet, muddy land

mate (MATE) the male or female partner of a pair of animals

predators (PRED-uh-turz) animals that live by hunting other animals for food

skeleton (SKEL-uh-tuhn) the framework of bones that supports and protects the body of an animal

territory (TER-uh-tor-ee) an area of land claimed by an animal

FIND OUT MORE

BOOKS

Dodson, Peter. *Triceratops Up Close: Horned Dinosaur*. Berkeley Heights, NJ: Enslow, 2011.

Mara, Wil. *Triceratops*. New York: Children's Press, 2012.

Rockwood, Leigh. *Triceratops*. New York: PowerKids Press, 2012.

WEB SITES

BBC Nature—Triceratops
www.bbc.co.uk/nature/life /Triceratops
Check out videos about *Triceratops* and other ancient animals.

National Geographic— Triceratops Horridus
http://animals.nationalgeographic .com/animals/prehistoric /triceratops-horridus
Learn more cool facts about *Triceratops*.

INDEX

ABOUT THE AUTHOR

Jennifer Zeiger lives in Chicago, Illinois. She writes and edits children's books on all sorts of topics.